Copyright © 2017 Jeff Stanton

ISBN: 1978172176
ISBN-13: 9781978172173

CONTENTS

TRUMP'S PSYCHOPATHY THREATENS THE INTERNAL STABILITY OF THE UNITED STATES AND THE WORLD

August 11, 2017

"In the early 1800s, doctors who worked with mental patients began to notice that some of their patients who appeared outwardly normal had what they termed a moral depravity or moral insanity, in that they seemed to possess no sense of ethics or of the rights of other people. The term psychopath was first applied to these people around 1900. The brains of psychopaths have been found to have weak connections among the components of the brain's emotional systems."—Psychology Today

"Psychopaths show a lack of emotion, especially the social emotions, such as shame, guilt, and embarrassment. Hervey Cleckley [one of the first to diagnose the sickness in 1941] said that the psychopaths he came into contact with showed a general poverty in major affective reactions and a lack of remorse or shame. The Psychopathy Checklist Revised (PCL-R) describes psychopaths as emotionally shallow and showing a lack of guilt. Psychopaths are notorious for their lack of fear. They show blame externalization, i.e., they blame others for events that are actually their fault. Glibness, superficial charm, untruthfulness, insincerity, impulsiveness, outright pathological lying and devaluing speech by inflating and distorting it toward selfish ends [are character traits]. The psychopath [is adept at] conning others for personal profit or pleasure. Cleckley spoke of his psychopaths showing a pathologic egocentricity [incapacity for love] and a parasitic lifestyle."—Psychology Today

President Donald Trump's pathological behavior at home is evidenced in his tweets and speeches. His communication with the "outside world" is typically acerbic and vengeful. His recent "fire and fury" threat to North Korea was belligerent, foolhardy and dangerous. The president simply does not understand, or care, that his words carry great weight. In this instance, financial markets around the world were rattled for a time. Moreover, Trump's biblical sounding threat came a day before the US dropped the second atomic bomb on Nagasaki.

Whether it's slamming media reports as fake news or calling a sitting US senator a hustler, Trump always aims to debase. His closeted racist agenda towards Muslims, Blacks and Latino's, and his preference for white cabinet members, will nullify some of the gains America has made to achieve a measure of racial and gender equality. His ring kissing political appointees, with the exception of a couple of Marines, are buffoons whose only mission is the decimation of the US federal government which they hope leads to profitable privatization for Wall Street.

Fear and white rage

Jeffrey St. Clair of Counter Punch looked into the Trump psyche. He has written two must-read pieces. One spends a bit of time deconstructing Trump as a father and husband.

Another looks at some of Trump's ignominious past. A gem from the latter piece is this:

"He sells fear and white rage, as if he has scented the rot eating away inexorably at the core of the System he helped construct. Of course, he still markets himself as the nation's top stud, the only figure man enough to eradicate the gravest threat to the Republic: Mexican immigrants. [This] is certainly a grandiose hypocrisy. The family fortune was built on immigrant labor. His father Fred boasted that his empire of suburban shacks was constructed by laborers 'right off the boat,' untainted by union membership. Donald followed the same reasoning at his own construction sites and in the low-wage jobs at his casinos and hotels."

Trump's political and governing psychopathy infects executive branch and a good metaphor for that is the creature in the movie Alien.

That monstrous "thing" is implanted into the actor John Hurt by a horseshoe crab-like critter that attaches itself to Hurt's face. It uses Hurt as a host, siphoning off his life for its own. Ultimately, the Alien explodes out of Hurt's chest/stomach area and scoots off somewhere into the spacecraft leaving Hurt dead. In the end, most of the crew of the spacecraft is killed by the fully grown creature.

Trump and most of his cronies exhibit the psychopathology of the Alien. They are slowly being implanted throughout the executive branch of the US government. They seek to eat away the guts of America's federal institutions, agencies and departments by spreading their acidic ideology into the Departments of Agriculture and Education. It acts on the morale and effectiveness of civil servants like the acid fluid that flows from the Alien, melting through metal and burning human flesh. Trump's 2018 budget is similar in purpose to the Alien's inner jaw that destroys it human prey, if it does not use the body as a host. Trump's draconian budget and his use of the Congressional Review Act are monstrous.

Take, for example, the Trump administration and the Department of Energy (DOE). The DOE is one of the most important units of the federal government. It is on the frontlines of protecting America from weapons of mass destruction and in securing the fragmented electrical grid that the country depends on. DOE funded Tesla with seed money early on through a program called E-ARPA when Wall Street would not.

Michael Lewis of Vanity Fair writes a chilling story describing Trump's political and ideological psychopathy at work in the $30 billion a year organization.

"The Trump people didn't seem to grasp, according to a former DOE employee, how much more than just energy the Department of Energy was about. They weren't totally oblivious to the nuclear arsenal, but even the nuclear arsenal didn't provoke in them much curiosity. 'They were just looking for dirt, basically,' said one of the people who briefed the Beachhead Team on national-security issues. 'What is the Obama administration not letting you do to keep the country safe?' The briefers were at pains to explain an especially sensitive aspect of national security: the United States no longer tests its nuclear weapons. Instead, it relies on physicists at three of the national labs—Los Alamos, Livermore, and Sandia—to simulate explosions, using old and decaying nuclear materials."

"[There were a] handful of young ideologues [sent to the Department of Energy] who called themselves the Beachhead Team. 'They mainly ran around the building insulting people,' says a former Obama official. 'There was a mentality that everything that government does is stupid and bad and the people are stupid and bad,' says another. They allegedly demanded to know the names and salaries of the 20 highest-paid people in the national-science labs overseen by the DOE. They'd eventually, according to former DOE staffers, delete the contact list with the e-mail addresses of all DOE funded scientists—apparently to make it more difficult for them to communicate with one another. 'These people were insane,' says the former DOE staffer. 'They weren't prepared. They didn't know what they were doing.'"

Lewis also noted in the Vanity Fair piece that the DOE was an agency that Rick Perry wanted to eliminate. Perry's role as head of the department has been ceremonial and bizarre, Lewis added.

Over here, over there

National security extends far beyond the US Department of Defense and the nation's intelligence agencies as a close study of the US Instruments of National Power show. The INPs are typically broken down into sensible categories: Diplomacy, Intelligence, Military, Economic, Financial, Law Enforcement, Information and human capital. Any one of them is powerful in its own right but they all overlap. No nation can match the INP's when they are used intelligently and in totality. That said, severely weakening or abusing any one of them can break the links that bind them together.

Take the INP Diplomacy, for example. Trump's sleepy Secretary of State Rex Tillerson seeks to eliminate many functions within the department through a 30 percent budget cut. One example of those reductions would be direct funding for quasi- and non-governmental organizations that serve niche missions, the Los Angeles Times reported. One group that will be hit is The American Jewish World Service who said much of its work would be jeopardized, according to the media report. The group fights poverty all over the world through 450 local organizations. Tillerson's State Dept. budget is a paltry $37.6 billion (in contrast Trump signed a $110 billion dollar arms deal with Saudi Arabia in May 2017).

Not listed specifically in the INPs is Education. Here too, Trump wants to cut out approximately 14 percent of the Department of Education's budget. That's just one salvo in the administration's quest to privatize public education. There is, perhaps, no more insidious program than the one to let public education systems die out across the land. If the Trump people get their way, the education system in the United States will become financially and racially segregated, again. All the INPs depend on a solid system of liberal and scientific education if the nation is to prosper. If the US does not take care of its people, and its infrastructure, the INPs weaken across the board as those left behind come to believe that there is no future for them (job, health insurance, roof over the head) in America. What's the point of their participation in a system that has left them as road kill? Trump cleverly preyed on these people for their votes, while Hillary Clinton decided they should rot.

False prophet: Trump

Trump is a false prophet. Those motivated to support him will come to understand that his psychopathy and his presence in the Oval Office will, if not checked, lead not to civil war, but a wicked malaise throughout the land. The nation will devolve into tribes: A military-industrial tribe, an evangelical tribe, a progressive tribe, tribes based on race and ethnicity, corporate tribes, or displaced tribes, wealthy tribes. In this scenario, tribes are stove-piped and rarely interact other than perhaps through trade. The tribes that make up the country become drug addled, not unlike the opioid epidemic underway, due in large part to unemployment and existential despair, according to Governing:

Governing.com reported that "It's not simply about the rise of a new class of addictive drugs that now take the lives of some 91 Americans every day. The opioid crisis is a jobs crisis; it's an affordable housing crisis. The same forces that have reshaped the economy over the past decade have left a void that's been filled, in many places, by opioids. A University of Pennsylvania study after last November's election found that President Trump had over performed in counties with the highest rates of 'deaths of despair,' which include suicide, drug overdose and alcohol poisoning. It supports the fact that there are many Americans who feel left behind by the changing economy, and who fundamentally don't believe the current political and policy framework is helping them."

Trump's two pronged national security strategy for the world seems to be this: Fire and fury and trade wars abroad, and incite domestic unrest at home. It is not all President Trump's fault, of course. He is what he is, a psychopath and a symptom of a country gone astray--at least for the moment.. In the end, Americans will come to realize they need to demand more of each other and those they elect to represent them. It is the American people who will need to set the ship back on course and get back to the Idea of America. In times of crisis, the United States tends to produce great leaders. Yet there is no one out there yet.

Jefferson said he thought a little revolution now and then is necessary. That revolution is here and it hurts. Americans need to get their s**t together.

UNITED STATES DROWNING IN AN OCEAN OF SUBJECTIVISM

July 25, 2017

"The very idea of freedom presupposes some objective moral law which overarches rulers and ruled alike. Subjectivism about values is eternally incompatible with democracy. We and our rulers are of one kind only so long as we are subject to one law. But if there is no Law of Nature, the ethos of any society is the creation of its rulers, educators and conditioners; and every creator stands above and outside his creation."—The Poison of Subjectivism, CS Lewis

"We should value those who solicit our votes by other standards than have recently been in fashion. While we believe that good is something to be invented, we demand of our rulers such qualities as "vision," "dynamism," "creativity," and the like. If we returned to the objective view we should demand qualities much rarer, and much more beneficial—virtue, knowledge, diligence and skill. Vision is for sale, or claims to be for sale, everywhere. But give me a man who will do a day's work for a day's pay, who will refuse bribes, who will not make up his facts, and who has learned his job."—The Poison of Subjectivism, CS Lewis

CS Lewis has a great point. Everywhere in the United States the disease of subjectivism is present. The evidence abounds: The polarization of the political system; the dismissal of history because of discomfort with historical facts; "trigger" warnings for literary texts that offend "sensibility"; the vicious censure befalling authors for developing literary characters of a different race or ethnic experience; applying the rules of law for some and not others; or disavowing a higher spiritual power of some sort. The digital maelstrom accelerates subjectivism.

Be forewarned that going forward, every individual and in-group in the United States is cautioned to stay in their own lane with their own histories. In this new American society, you run the danger of being pilloried if you express an opinion outside your own individual/in-group reality. The reasoning goes something like this: "You weren't there, how can you have an opinion on that?" The response might be, "Sure, I wasn't around when Alexander the

Great was rampaging across the world, but I have some opinion based on studies I've done." And the response you're likely to get these days is, "No good, you are not Macedonian."

Make America what?

Subjectivism calls into question the very notion of what it means to be an American. Is there such a thing as the United States? What does anyone have in common any longer? It is as if "the educators, conditioners and creators," that Lewis refers to, have tried to apply the Many World's Theory from Quantum Mechanics in creating and managing society, a society in which all possible outcomes are sought and all outcomes are obtained, each in a different world/reality that only you and your in-group are aware of.

In this new American society "reality" exists at two different poles. One reality seeks shelter in its own individual/ingroup world and is content to live a two dimensional life as described in Edwin Abbott Abbott's Flatland. They are not aware that they are being manipulated by realities at the other end of the pole and shun those who posit that such manipulation exists or even in the reality of other worlds.

At the other pole exists a "reality" in which the individual/in-group are able to create ever more realities in which compasses show no direction, alternative histories exist and problems/issues are dealt with by wiping one reality out for another. Every day is new, yesterday is forgotten, fads and technology appear and disappear, politicians and corporate heads sell vision and disruption, you create your own news and reality; and, well, hubris leads humanity to believe it is the highest order species in any world or universe.

Excess and passivity

According to William James in his lecture The Dilemma of Determinism, "Subjectivism everywhere fosters the fatalistic mood of mind. It makes those who are already too inert more passive still; it renders wholly reckless those whose energy is already in excess. All through history we find how subjectivism, as soon as it has a free career, exhausts itself in every sort of spiritual, moral, and practical license. Its optimism turns to an ethical indifference, which infallibly brings dissolution in its train. It transforms life from a tragic reality into an insincere melodramatic exhibition, as foul or as tawdry as anyone's diseased curiosity pleases to carry it out."

"I have heard a graduate of this very school express in the pulpit his willingness to sin like David, if only he might repent like David. You may tell me he was only sowing his wild, or rather his tame, oats; and perhaps he was. But the point is that in the subjectivistic oat-sowing, wild or tame, it becomes a systematic necessity and the chief function of life. After the pure and classic truths, the exciting and rancid ones must be experienced; and if the stupid virtues of the philistine herd do not then come in and save society from the influence of the children of light, a sort of inward putrefaction becomes its inevitable doom."

Subjectivism will destroy the country unless some commonalities are agreed upon to unite America. Who doesn't long, as CS Lewis said, for "Virtue, knowledge, diligence and skill. Vision is for sale, or claims to be for sale, everywhere. But give me a man who will do a day's work for a day's pay, who will refuse bribes, who will not make up his facts, and who has learned his job."

This is no call for a return to the "good old days" in which slavery, racism, anti-LGBTQ, and a "woman's place in the kitchen" were widespread in practice. What is needed is a set of beliefs or fundamentals that all citizens in the USA—human beings—can adhere too to find common bond. There must be ideals, codes that go beyond crass alliances that seek to cut taxes or undercut healthcare for the young and the old. Americans need to get out of their lanes and take care of each other.

As it stands now, it seems that Americans have segregated themselves into stovepipes, as if by some sort of invisible hand. What follows that is distasteful. Lewis warned that subjectivism is the mother of fascism. The "F" word is on a lot of people's minds these days as authoritarian leadership seems to be on the upswing not only in the United States, but elsewhere in the world. New realities are, indeed, being created.

"Many a popular 'planner' on a democratic platform, many a mild-eyed scientist in a democratic laboratory means, in the last resort, just what the Fascist means. He believes that "good" means whatever men are conditioned to approve. He believes that it is the function of him and his kind to condition men; to create consciences by eugenics, psychological manipulation of infants, state education and mass propaganda. Because he is confused, he does not yet fully realize that those who create conscience cannot be subject to conscience themselves. But he must awake to the logic of his position sooner or later; and when he does, what barrier remains between us and the final division of the race into a few conditioners who stand themselves outside morality and the many conditioned in whom such morality as the experts choose is produced at the experts' pleasure?"—CS Lewis

TRUMP, REPUBLICANS SEEK TO EUTHANIZE 80 MILLION YOUNG AND OLD AMERICANS: DEMOCRATS WILL BE ACCESSORIES TO THE CRIME

June 30, 2017

"These county lessons are significant because Medicaid is the largest funder of preventive health, births/pregnancy, drug recovery and mental health treatment services. When we talk about the growing costs of Medicaid, it is prudent to remember the population being served. Of the 80 million individuals covered by Medicaid today, more than 34 million are children under 18 years old, 7.3 million are low-income elderly and 11 million are disabled. Approximately one-third are very low-income adults between ages 19 and 64, yet these same adults account for less than 16 percent of Medicaid costs. By comparison, the elderly and disabled represent 61 percent of Medicaid costs, with children at around 20 percent. In fact, 50 percent of all U.S. births are covered by Medicaid."—Matthew D. Chase, executive director of the National Association of Counties.

"Low income people—an estimated 23 million—will be stripped of all health coverage. Millions of people will suffer needlessly, and many thousands will die an early death. For the authors of these bills and their corporate backers, this is not an unfortunate byproduct, but the deliberate aim of their health care reform. For the richest 10 percent who tower above the lower orders and control the political system and its two major parties, the diversion of money from profits and private bank accounts to keep working people alive and reasonably healthy—especially those too old to serve as a source of surplus value and profit—is an intolerable affront. Life expectancy in America is already declining and mortality rates are rising for the working class, in tandem with the colossal growth of social inequality. The ruling class wants to accelerate this process."—Barry Grey and Kate Randall, World Socialist Website.

Who, exactly, are the people that the Republicans in the US Congress represent? Or, should we ask, do they have the best interests of their local constituents in mind? If constituents mean insurance companies, donors and the financial gods they worship, then they are wonderful representatives. They are doing what their masters seek and could be the elimination of 80 million non-economically productive old, disabled and young Americans who rely on Medicaid.

Eating their own

It is difficult to comprehend why Republican voters are so inclined to watch as their fellow citizens are likely to be cut off from the lifeline that is Medicaid. It is more appalling, I suppose, to see the Democrats and their constituents standing by and not fight the Trump-Republican madness, offering no plan and playing it safe in hopes of winning congressional seats in the 2018 elections. In fact, they seem willing to sacrifice those 80 million Americans just to retain their House and Senate seats.

If Americans who identify as Republicans—and, by their silence, Democrats—are willing to kill off, or cause the suffering of so many of their fellow citizens, what does that say about the state of the United States? We are told repeatedly that the economic recovery is on track, unemployment is down, and the stock market is setting records every month. But you would not think that after visiting many of America's cities, rural areas and many small communities. And now comes word from America's economic and political overlords that there are not enough qualified employees in America to fill positions that are available. Who is to blame for that? Why, of course, the "little people," not the financial and ideological savages who are ripping apart the country.

To force the minions to become qualified, Republicans and Democrats seek to privatize the entire US education system, ensuring that corporate teachers will train "we the people" to become qualified for this and that job. But that will create two societies in the United States: One in which 30 percent of Americans fill all the "good" jobs and are gated off in their own communities protected by private security companies. The other 70 percent will include homeless tribes, squatters, the unemployed, the sick, the non-productive, and those 80 million Americans dumped off Medicaid. But, hey! For an $800 billion tax cut for the wealthy—thanks to crippling Medicaid—what is a few million unproductive lives?

If euthanasia became acceptable across the land, Trump and his Republican money changers would likely pass legislation containing mandates for staying alive just to bolster productivity, health and taxable income. The Democrats would shrug their shoulders.

Thanks a lot!

But the fact is that the American people are the nation's most important infrastructure. But with each passing day, they are being subjected to death on the installment plan. It took a few decades for the financial cannibals to eat away at the social programs produced by Franklin D. Roosevelt and Lyndon Johnson. It seems odd that President Jimmy Carter kicked off the effort.

"In 1978, Jimmy Carter released the United States' first comprehensive national urban policy, A New Partnership to Conserve America's Communities. With its emphasis on voluntarism, decentralization, and public–private partnerships, the national urban policy accelerated the devolution of social policy begun under the Nixon Administration and laid the foundation for Reagan's retrenchment. Looking beyond the urban policy deliberations to the activities of two other Carter initiatives, the National Commission on Neighborhoods and the White Conference on Balanced Growth and National Economic Development, demonstrates that state and local officials and neighborhood advocates were complicit in establishing and legitimating urban policies predicated on privatization and devolution." (Privatization, Devolution, and Jimmy Carter's National Urban Policy)

Ronald Reagan, George H.W. Bush, Bill Clinton, George W. Bush and Barak Obama took the baton from Carter and continued the slow torture of American society. Trump has eagerly grabbed that baton. Now, the country is notably more vicious, partisan, politically paralyzed, at war, confused and, in some segments of the population, afraid. (As an aside, I was walking past an Indian family seated on benches in a park. There were five of them with two being teenagers. I overheard one of the adults and the two teenagers talking about being deported. "Where would we go," one teenager asked. Another said, "You are from here, they won't deport you." (Thanks, President Donald J. Trump!)

On June 26, the US Supreme Court weighed in on Trump's travel ban. The court ruled that, absent a foreign national's demonstrated connection to someone in the United States (family, employer, etc.), the person would not be allowed into the country. The Supreme Court was to hear the case in

October 2017 but recent Court of Appeals decisions opting into some of Trump's travel ban have taken effect. Just so.

Fight them there to protect the dystopia here

Pentagon officials are fond of saying that the world is the most volatile that they've seen in their careers. Indeed it is, and they need look no further than their own homeland where in Las Vegas a gunman killed 58 and injured scores more. Perhaps a good analogy for the internal political, social and cultural dynamic of the United States homeland is the melting and crumbling ice sheets in West Antarctica. Scientists say there are "natural" processes at work on the ice sheets. Can we say that "natural" historical processes are at work that are fracturing the American Republic? Is Trump the political version of climate change?

Trump and the Republicans—and their partners in crime the Democrats—are accelerating the crackup of the American Republic. Trump's people are unrepentant liars, no more so than Trump himself or maybe Sarah Sanders, Trump's press secretary. Disaster follows in Trump's wake. The Boeing plant that Trump visited is dumping 200 workers. Saudi Arabia, with Trump's support, seeks to turn Qatar into a Saudi protectorate. The Saudi's, Egypt and the UAE have in place an economic embargo of Qatar underway that Trump supports. The Middle East and Persian Gulf countries seem to be headed for more violence, if that is possible. And now, the US is engaging in combat action against Syrian government forces that are supported by Russian and Iranian military forces. If that were not enough, Trump plans to reject elements of the nuke deal with Iran.

That's all, folks!

Blood is flowing from the US Constitution, the Bill of Rights and the Declaration of Independence. Lingchi, or death by 1,000 cuts, is the Republican's preferred method for turning the American Republic into a corporate and security state, while culling the non-productive human herd in America.

We were all taught as young kids that it was better to fight the bad guys over "there" instead of "here." But what if "here" turns into a dystopian republic as portrayed in the novels We, Brave New World, and 1984? What if we are,

God forbid, headed towards a version of Syria and Iraq?

So many years have passed since George W. Bush was president. I thought that was a dangerous time, and it was. But Trump and the Republicans—and their woeful Democratic "opponents"—have taken wickedness to a new levels of savageness. Civil rights enforcement is in jeopardy with Jeff Sessions as attorney general. The butchers in the Office of Management and Budget and Treasury could care less about 70 percent of the country's populace. The Trump administration is nearly lily white in a land filled with Black, Brown, Yellow and LGBTQ populations.

The only cabinet member worth his weight in salt is Defense Secretary Jim Mattis. His sole mission is to support American Marines, soldiers, sailors and airmen. Under his watch, open celebrations in the Pentagon for Black, Brown, Hispanic, LGBTQ and First Peoples.

Many say after an article like this, well, that's nice, but what is your solution? The answer to that is in an article I wrote on July 25, 2005. I think it still applies 12 years later. Civil justice groups need to build seamless cross-cultural and political networks in communities around the land. If no new political party can be created, then the Democrats must be retrained to represent the people.

Maybe it would help if people stopped looking down into their mobile devices and take a look at the world around them and act.

MASS INCARCERATION, PRISON LABOR IN THE UNITED STATES

June 21, 2017

The Federal Prison Industries (FPI) under the brand UNICORE operates approximately 52 factories within prisons across the United States. Prisoners manufacture or assemble a number of products for the US military, homeland security, and federal agencies according to the UNICORE/FPI website. They produce furniture, clothing and circuit boards, in addition to providing computer aided design services and call center support for private companies.

UNICORE/FPI makes a pitch for employing its call center support personnel for firms thinking about offshoring their call center functions. The logic is that, hey!, they may be prisoners, but it's keeping the jobs in the USA that matters. Fair enough. That approach cuts out the middlemen and women who are often desperate for any kind of work but, through no fault of their own, are not behind prison bars and employable by UNICORE/FPI.

There are any number of angles to take on why the USA is the world's number one incarcerator: Capitalism, racism, social and political injustice, a pay-as-you-go legal system, bone-headed policy makers, prison lobbyists, the death penalty, employment/unemployment, drugs, gangs, costs/prices for basic goods, and a host of behavioral, psychological and environmental issues that I have missed.

But inevitably it's the black hole of money that eventually sucks in and corrupts everyone from local communities in need of the work a prison facility provides to those investors who profit from the prison industry. Even anti-death penalty advocates and reformers for prison justice groups have to have cash. They earn their livelihoods and profit from the misery and labor squeezed from imprisoned human property.

For the love of money

From October 2016 through March 2017, UNICORE/FPI sold $252,414,987 million worth of goods and services. The prison labor industry is very keen on promoting its role in assembling the US military's widely used Single Channel

Ground and Airborne Radio System (SINCGARS). In January defense contractor Harris Corp. was awarded a $403 million contract by the US Defense Logistics Agency for spare parts supporting tactical radio systems, which includes SINCGARS.

"UNICOR/FPI is a major supplier of SINCGARS radios, mounts, antennas, and installation and repair kits and when hard-mounted, our SINCGARS equipment meets rigorous military standards for shock and vibration in aircraft and tactical vehicles, such as Bradley's and Humvees. Through our nationwide network of factories and trained technicians, we have successfully met aggressive production and distribution needs for this crucial communication equipment in Middle East military operations."

Some of the purchases by the US Department of Defense include $14.8 million for electronic components, $887 thousand for communications equipment, $26.7 million for office furniture, $27.1 million for special purpose clothing and $7.5 million for body armor. The Department of Homeland security spent $372,255 on administrative support. The Executive Office of the US President spent $389 for signs and identification plates.

Fight fire with inmates

According to a Mother Jones article in 2015, somewhere between 30 and 40 percent of California's forest firefighters are state prison inmates with some 4,000 working at any one time on fire lines. So dependent on the inmates was California that prison reforms that would see the release of some of the incarcerated firefighters were put on hold for fear of losing the manpower to fight California blazes. Then California Attorney General Kamala Harris, now a US Senator, was behind the effort to keep the "cheap" firefighters behind bars,

"Prison reform advocates have raised concerns that the state is so reliant on the cheap labor of inmate firefighters that policymakers may be slow to adopt prison reforms as a result. The concern was magnified last fall, when lawyers for state Attorney General Kamala Harris argued that extending an early prison-release program to "all minimum custody inmates at this time would severely impact fire camp participation—a dangerous outcome while California is in the middle of a difficult fire season and severe drought." Harris has since said she was "troubled" by the argument, and the state has ruled that minimum custody inmates, including firefighters, are eligible for the program so long as it proves not to deplete the numbers of inmate firefighters."

US Immigration and Customs Enforcement detains women, men, children, and LGBTQI individuals in over 200 county jails and for-profit prisons, according to the grassroots group CIVIC. Some of these individuals include legal permanent residents with longstanding family and community ties, asylum-seekers, and victims of human trafficking.

It was former President Bill Clinton (Democrat) who started to load up detention centers and jails with immigrants, CIVIC noted. "In 1996, President Bill Clinton signed the Antiterrorism and Effective Death Penalty Act (AEDPA) and the Illegal Immigration Reform and Immigrant Responsibility Act (IIRIRA), which doubled the number of people in immigration detention from 8,500 each day in 1996 to 16,000 in 1998. Today, the detention population has increased fourfold to approximately 34,000 individuals each day, due in part to a congressionally mandated lock-up quota"

President Donald Trump's (Republican) animosity to immigrants is well known. He and his aptly named attorney general, Jefferson Beauregard Sessions, will make sure detention centers and prisons are overfilled with men, women and children from Mexico, Central and South America. Trump and Session's maniacal quest wage war on crime, drugs and terrorism will likely ensure that many thousands more will find themselves locked away and working for UNICORE/FPI or, through imprisonment, continue to line the pockets of private prison company owners. In a classic case of "contradiction" such prisons will help increase local community employment and provide other economic benefits.

Immigrants too

The non-profit group Towards Justice reported that a lawsuit is moving forward pitting immigrants who were forced into labor while in detention against a private prison corporation.

"For the first time in history, a federal court allowed a class of immigrant detainees to jointly proceed with forced labor claims against the country's second-largest private prison provider. Judge Kane in the District of Colorado certified a class of between 50,000 and 60,000 current and former immigrant detainees held at GEO's Aurora, Colorado detention facility since 2004. These individuals, some of whom were found to legally reside in this country after months in detention, allege that they were forced to clean the detention center without pay and under threat of solitary confinement. This practice allowed GEO to reduce labor costs at the Aurora facility, where it employs just one custodian to maintain a detention center that houses up to 1,500 people at a time."

Everyone has their hands in the pie

In January 2017, the Prison Policy Initiative (prisonpolicy.org) worked up a study titled Following the Money of Mass Incarceration. It shines the light on some of the unsettling reasons why the United States will never be able to reduce its. significantly, its mass incarceration rates. Those who depend on money that the prison industry provides will never give it up. It's not just private companies but local communities (as mentioned above), bondsmen, unions all the way up to the US Department of Defense that collect fees or purchase UNICORE/FPI products and services at dirt cheap prices.

"Bail bond companies that collect $1.4 billion in nonrefundable fees from defendants and their families actively work to block reforms that threaten its profits, even if reforms could prevent people from being detained in jail because of their poverty. Specialized phone companies win monopoly contracts and charge families up to $24.95 for a 15-minute phone call. Commissary vendors that sell goods to incarcerated people—who rely largely on money sent by loved ones—is an even larger industry that brings in $1.6 billion a year. 38 towns and cities in the U.S., more than 10% of all revenue is collected from court fines and fees. In St. Louis County, five towns generated more than 40% of their annual revenue from court fines and fees in 2013."

The over-incarceration of Americans is just one more vexing issue, piled on many—Afghanistan, Syria, Iran, education, Trump, health care, taxes, mass shootings, weather disasters—in which US citizens find themselves trapped on the right or left and can't bring themselves to cross dividing lines and work, civically and with civility, together.

WITCHES BREW: TERRORISM, GHOSTS OF VIETNAM, ETERNAL WAR

June 7, 2017

Coincident to the Pentagon's request for thousands more US soldiers to be shipped off to Afghanistan comes the massive vehicle borne improvised explosive device (VBID) attack in Kabul that killed nearly 100 and wounded 400 others. Among the wounded are said to be about a dozen US citizens who, likely, are diplomatic/defense and support contractors. The Taliban vehemently denied any involvement in the attack. The Islamic State is a likely suspect. Meanwhile in London, during the first weekend in June, terrorists there driving a van mowed down pedestrians and then went about stabbing random victims. The result? 7 dead, 21 critically wounded. (Update: the Las Vegas gunman killed 58 and wounded scores more. The Pentagon's request for more troops was approved and it will send roughly 4000 more soldiers on top of the 11000 already there.)

And so the world is off to the races again with a news cycle that features the routine victim portrayals, on scene interviews, expert analysis, and statements from leaders around the world condemning the attacks and vowing to carry the fight to the evildoers. The UK prime minister, Theresa May, calls now for Internet censorship and President Trump wants the US judicial branch to vacate its role as a check and on the executive branch. As to May's worry about the terrorists using the Internet to exploit weaknesses, the issue was brought up 15 years ago in an American Behavioral Scientist piece, titled Terror in Cyberspace, Terrorists Will Exploit and Widen the Gap Between Governing Structures and the Public, in which scenarios explored have come to life today.

So we all watch the carnage on television or the Internet and empathize for, maybe, 10 minutes. Then, we get back to the daily grind of work, soap operas, video games, sporting events, the mobile device and the Game of Thrones television series. We know that more attacks are sure to come. We civilized 21st Century world citizens have become accustomed to civilian, military and enemy body counts on television, in the papers, on the Internet, and in conversation. We call it the new normal, but it us anything but: The Internet-World Wide Web and telecommunications networks have not so clearly changed the world, as much as it has provided a mirror to the savagery of the human species. Whether it is terrorism, toxic destruction of the Earth, collateral damage, poisoned water, austerity, or man-made famine, those woes have always existed but now we can see them unfolding 24/7 on cable news, Twitter and Facebook. It hurts and then it numbs.

This has all the feel of the Vietnam War Era during which political, social, cultural and racial/economic currents came together like three overflowing rivers. It seems some form of that may happen again. It may take years, but it seems to be coming.

Mini-Tet Offensives

The Kabul attack, and to a lesser extent the London, UK, event, became props to support the Pentagon's request for more US troops to support operations in Afghanistan. The Pentagon has repeatedly asserted that is is losing in Afghanistan and observers are hard pressed to see how 4000 more US troops can change what has stymied US military planners for 16 years, not to mention getting the Afghan security forces to fight.

How are a few thousand US soldiers sent to and fro to Afghanistan going to bring the Taliban to its knees or stop terrorist attacks from happening anywhere in the world? Even as the Islamic State is being squashed in Iraq and Syria, they are able to create havoc in Baghdad, Kabul, the Philippines, London/Manchester, UK, and on the World Wide Web.

Don't we need 500,000 plus soldiers in Afghanistan as we did in Vietnam to crush the adversaries? Why the incremental increases? Why not seek the services of 1 million American citizens via the draft to go and get the job done in Afghanistan, Iraq, Yemen and Syria?

The suicide attacks that ISIS is so adept at serve as mini-Tet Offensives: They remind world leaders and military planners that they are largely helpless to eliminate terrorist attacks. The relatively low numbers of reinforcements requested by the Pentagon are puzzling. If the US wanted to annihilate the Taliban and the Islamic State, they'd get the Whole of American Society involved in the task. Not that they haven't tried. But most Americans don't care about US military actions in Afghanistan, Iraq or Syria. Nor do they want to go to war with Iran, which Trump seems keen to do.

Censoring the Internet is no solution. Want to stop terrorists and uncover propaganda? How about a basic education in critical thinking merging liberal arts and general science? Or maybe reduce war-making. As it is we are heading to a situation where we will not have one Vietnam War, but many: North Korea, Iraq, Syria, Yemen, Somalia, etc. And then there is the matter of active shooters in the United States.

The Haunting

In a New York Times article dated August 7, 1967, two unidentified generals were quoted, one who stated that he had destroyed a single North Vietnamese division three times: "I've chased main-force units all over the country and the impact was zilch. It meant nothing to the people. Unless a more positive and more stirring theme than simple anti-communism can be found, the war appears likely to go on until someone gets tired and quits, which could take generations."

The other general's quote was this: "Every time Westmorland makes a speech about how good the South Vietnam Army is, I want to ask him why he keeps calling for more Americans. His need for reinforcements is a measure of our failure with the Vietnamese."

Replace the "anti-communism and Vietnamese" with the Taliban, Islamic State or any terrorist group and the sentiments from 1967 are relevant in 2017.

American society appears culturally fragmented and stove-piped in three factions: Left, right and center. This is not dissimilar to the late 1960s and early 1970s. Aggressive Alt-Righter's have taken up the mantel of Neo-White Nationalism, an ideology that finds friends in a Republican White House and Justice Department Attorney General Jefferson Sessions.

The Democrat Left still bemoans Hillary Clinton's loss to Trump in 2016 and has, as yet, no aggressive platform to counter the Alt-Right or appeal to its lost followers. The Independent Center looks Left and Right and disdains the rigid, uncompromising ideology they hold. If the stovepipes crack open in the worst way, the streets are where passions will be fought for as they were during the Vietnam era.

Vietnam

There are other similarities to the Vietnam experience. President Donald Trump's administration is in disarray and under investigation by the US Justice Department. CNN reports that former FBI Director James Comey will testify in the US Senate that Trump pressured him to halt the investigation into Russian influence operations during the 2016 presidential race (update: he did.). The country is already, officially, a nation at war by presidential decree, and is even flirting with a war against North Korea. To top it off, Trump just declared war on the planet on June 1 by withdrawing from the Paris Climate Accords. Weekly reports of Russian propaganda operations appear in the Washington Post and New York Times.

The Trump administration is cornered and dangerous.

It's hard not to draw comparisons with the Vietnam War experience. The convergence of the anti-war and anti-racism movements, the criminal investigations of President Richard Nixon, and a cultural sea change challenging the established order was, then, unprecedented. Its ghosts seem to be haunting the American Republic at this moment in time.

According to History.com: "Though US. and South Vietnamese forces managed to hold off the Tet Offensive Communist attacks, news coverage of the offensive (including the lengthy Battle of Hue) shocked and dismayed the American public and further eroded support for the war effort. Despite heavy casualties, North Vietnam achieved a strategic victory with the Tet Offensive, as the attacks marked a turning point in the Vietnam War and the beginning of the slow, painful American withdrawal from the region."

History does repeat itself simply because humans are repetitive creatures.

"And corruption is stranglin' the land. The police force is watching the people and the people just can't understand. We don't know how to mind our own business, 'cause the whole world's got to be just like us. Now we are fighting a war over there but no matter who's the winner we can't pay the cost."—Steppenwolf Monster, 1969.

SAY A PRAYER FOR THE HOMELESS, TRUMP'S PEOPLE WILL NOT

May 23, 2017

It is a bright sunny day in the Washington, DC, metropolitan region. The sky is clear blue and the air is cool. It's definitely a windows-down driving day as I get in my '99 Camaro and set off to work from Arlington, Virginia, to 16th and K Street in downtown Washington. It is just about six miles to get from home, near the Pentagon and Fort Myer, to the office.

It's a pretty standard commute today, stop and go traffic. My path takes me past the US Marine Corps Memorial in Virginia, an awesome piece of art that still motivates me. I'm now turning onto the ramp that takes me to the Roosevelt Bridge across the Potomac River. Above the ramp is a highway overpass/underpass.

The traffic slows to a stop and I find myself on the road directly below the overpass/underpass which signals I've crossed into Washington, DC's jurisdiction. I'm daydreaming but look to my left and up to a section of the overpass/underpass and see that a homeless person (HP) has made a home of sorts. There are blankets, sleeping bags and plastic sheets placed tightly next to each other that hang from the supporting beams. They stretch down in a semicircle around the flat space up under the underpass. It's a wall that offers the HP some measure of relief from the elements and onlookers like me. There is junk scattered on either side of the HP's home: A broken exercise bench and dilapidated, busted bicycle among the items. Plastic bags hang from the beams, an obvious attempt to make it more difficult for the rats to gain access to the bag's contents.

Home sweet home

Traffic is moving now and up ahead is an HP who has a sign that reads "Thank You." Someone ahead of me has given him a bottle of water and he is grateful. I slow down and hand him a dollar asking, "Do you live up there, referring to the home I just passed. The HP says, "Oh, no, that's not mine, I live down there," as he signals to another overpass/underpass in the distance.

I'm on Roosevelt Bridge now, bobbing and weaving between cars as I make my way to the farthest lane. As I cross the Potomac I see the Washington Monument in the distance and to my left is the John F. Kennedy Center. My mind wanders to the scenes in the horrifying Zapruder film. Then comes visions of Malcolm X, Robert Kennedy and Martin Luther King. I shake my head. Reminders of the past are everywhere. I ask myself what the USA would have been like if they lived. But better pay attention to the traffic.

Now I'm making a slow left turn onto a ramp that will put me on the E Street Express. I notice to my left another HP. He's lying down on top of a concrete slab reading a book. He is covered by is a large blue plastic tarp. His 'place' rests between two concrete barriers in a grassy area. As I make the hard left, slowly though, I notice the gaudy Institute of Peace building on my right. Looking left I see a small tent nestled in among some bushes off the ramp. What's the deal?

E Street

I'm on the E Street Expressway now. I look up to my left and see the Saudi Embassy. Looking down a bit I see a wall painted with some pretty cool graffiti. Panning down, I notice three small tents in a grassy area. I'm just about to the Georgetown and K Street intersection. The famed Watergate building is very close. As I make the turn to get to K Street, I see ten tents: It's a mini HP tent community. There is a guy with a pit bull and its puppies. There's a campfire that's going strong. Some guys are sitting around it. Garbage is scattered around some of the tents. Some other guys are cleaning up around their homes. To the left and right are HP's holding signs that say, "Help." Looking to the right I notice more tents set below an underpass. And as I move along, I see a couple of tents on a nearby hill.

At the Georgetown and K Street intersection are more HPs. One has a dog and sits on a lawn chair on the median strip asking for help. There is a woman on another median strip asking for cash. To my right is a gentleman shaking a McDonald's plastic cup with change in it. His home consists of two shopping carts full of blankets and who knows what. And there is a guy holding a sign, "Anything will help. God bless."

Making a right onto K Street I notice that there are some very expensive town and apartment homes. Behind me rests Georgetown, where Washington's power elite dine and play. I'm pretty close to my place of work. A few blocks and stoplights and I'm there. I'm in the lead position in the right hand lane at a stoplight now. To my left and across the street is another shopping cart loaded with dirty blankets and personal belongings. A minute or two ago, I passed a sidewalk with a mattress, door and lamp: Another HP home.

Bipolar

I'm pulling into the parking garage now absorbing the bipolar reality I've seen. On this particular day, I stay later than usual. It's about 8 PM. I head out of the building and turn to go to the garage and almost walk into a small red tent abutting a building. A snoring sound from someone inside can be heard. This is 16th and K in Washington, DC, I mutter to myself.

The view on the return trip home to Arlington is the same. I notice on this route that the mini-HP tent city is very close to four older but high priced townhomes that sit, stranded almost, across from a gas station, itself across from the Watergate.

I leave Washington, DC, with a sense of urgency. I look forward to getting back to Arlington, one of the top communities in America to live, work and raise a family. I decide to stop at the 7–11 market located just about at the intersection of the bustling Columbia Pike and Walter Reed Drive. The 7–11 is adjacent to a 24/7 McDonald's and a host of bars and restaurants.

Thank Heaven for 7–11

I'm in the parking lot of 7–11 now which is about 500 meters from my house. Out of the car I go. I'm looking forward to getting some beer and salted peanuts and getting to the comfort of my own home. As I walk in, I notice a HP. I also recognize the face. It's a kid I used coach in high school contact football. I give him what cash I have, not much, and figure I'll use my credit card for my stuff and buy him something to eat. And there's another HP sidling up to me asking if I have any more money. I tell him I can get him a sandwich but that's about it.

The homeless have been appearing frequently in Arlington and I expect in a lot of other communities around the nation too. The politicians and "experts" talk about enforcing drug laws and the scourge of opiates and heroin until they are blue in the face.

The epidemic that is the increase in homeless persons, young and old, should frighten every American. They remind most of the "lucky us" with mortgages and debt (used for cheap goods and services, not extravagance) that we are only a half dozen missed paychecks and loss of health insurance away from living in a tent. Moving in with other family members is a 1920s option, not available these days. Who wants to burden the kids?. Trump's people seek to eliminate Social Security and de-federalize safety net programs and dump them on the States, most of which have debt problems of their own. It is a callous Pontius Pilate move.

Trump and his administration are to the federal government, poor and middle classes what the Islamic State is to Christians and Shia. Trump's followers and supporters are every bit as radical in their ideology as Daesh is in theirs. Their souls are corrupt. As an aside, those hoping Trump is moved out of the presidency should note that Vice President Pence is an evangelical Christian who rejects the theory of evolution. Mike Pence is a creationist.

The ttwo political parties are not going to make America great again. Democrats and Republicans, alt-right, alt-left, conservatives/liberals will not help the country if they stick to their given brand names. The system has been twisted by them all. A country before agency, party and ambition attitude has to emerge in America. If that does not happen soon, war in the streets will surely come at some point.

America's homeless nomads serve as a message from the future, a dystopian one in which tens of millions wander the countryside living off the land. Many will establish their own tent cities. Some homeless people turn into well-armed militias. And the future will be that way because we, as a people, refused to put country above all else.

Saying a prayer for the homeless is saying one for all of us.

TRUMP'S TRAITOR, POMPEO'S FRAUD, THE DAMNED: CHELSEA MANNING GOES FREE, JULIAN ASSANGE AND ED SNOWDEN DOOMED

May 17, 2017

Pompeo's Fraud

Chelsea Manning's leaked information made WikiLeaks and its founder, Julian Assange, a household name. It also made them permanent enemies of the US State. In 2010, Assange released a video that he called Collateral Murder. The video showed an airstrike in which Iraqi journalists are killed. Other releases based on Manning's leak were known as the Afghan Diary and Iraq War Logs. The diplomatic cables exposed some of the silly machinations of the US State Department and the over classification of documents.

Meanwhile, mainstream media (MSM) outlets like the New York Times and Washington Post feasted on the leaks and gave them prominent coverage daily, even as they excoriated Assange and his merry band of leakers. The MSM believes that WikiLeaks is not "real" journalism even as they used the classified material Assange provided to bolster their subscription numbers. Aren't they accessories to Assange's crime? Apparently not.

Assange has been living for the past five years under diplomatic protection in the Embassy of Ecuador in the United Kingdom. He has been accused of rape in Sweden (since dropped) and, if he leaves the embassy, would be arrested by UK authorities and, ultimately, end up in the USA. To make matters worse, now he is a target of the Central Intelligence Agency (CIA) director. Pompeo once praised WikiLeaks. Whatever data he has seen that made him go ballistic can't be good for Assange, obviously. Attorney General Jefferson Beauregard Sessions over at the Justice Department has hinted that an arrest warrant is in the works.

He will never get a get out of jail card and is trapped in Ecuador's Embassy in London. The trip from the UK to Sweden to the USA would be swift if he capitulates. "It's time to call out WikiLeaks for what it really is: A non-state, hostile intelligence service often abetted by state actors like Russia," CIA director Mike Pompeo said at a May event hosted by the Center for Strategic and International Studies in Washington, DC. "Assange is a narcissist who has created nothing of value and he relies on the dirty work of others to make himself famous: He's a fraud."

Assange continues to dig a hole for himself with the recent CIA Vault leaks even as he enlightens us all, apparently, about the machinations of governments around the world.

Manning: Trump's traitor

Trans woman Army soldier Chelsea Manning was released today from the US Disciplinary Barracks at Fort Leavenworth, thanks to former President Barack Obama's merciful commutation of Manning's 35-year sentence.

"The sentence she received was very disproportionate relative to what other leakers had received," Obama was quoted as saying by the Los Angeles Times during a press conference in January. "I feel very comfortable that justice has been served and that a message [to those who would leak classified information] has still been sent."

On January 26, President Donald Trump said that Manning was an ungrateful traitor and should have served out her prison sentence, according to Trump's Twitter account.

Sometime in early 2010 Army soldier Bradley Manning, an intelligence analyst stationed in Iraq, surreptitiously leaked to WikiLeaks scores of classified material. Included were US State Department diplomatic cables, videos of US Army operations and airstrikes in Iraq and Afghanistan, and other sensitive Army reports some detailing activities at Guantanamo Bay.

Manning was arrested in July 2010 and subsequently imprisoned at a US Marine Corps brig in the state of Virginia. She was court-martialed and subsequently was convicted on 17 charges, including espionage, in legal proceedings known as the United States versus Manning. Manning had served seven years of her sentence when on January 17, 2017, Obama pardoned her.

The presiding judge in United States versus Manning reduced the 35-year sentence by 112 days because of the solitary confinement she underwent while at the Marine Corps jail. She attempted suicide twice while at the Fort Leavenworth prison.

Chelsea Manning's court-martial verdict has been appealed by her lawyers, according to a published report on MSN.com. Until a military court makes a decision on her case, she will continue to receive health benefits after leaving prison. She will be an active duty, unpaid Army soldier with the rank of private.

"For the first time, I can see a future for myself as Chelsea," Manning said in a May 9 statement released through the American Civil Liberties Union. "I can imagine surviving and living as the person who I am and can finally be in the outside world."

One of Manning's income sources after her release will be speaking fees and a likely book deal and movie. She is registered with AllAmericanSpeakers.com and the website has a portfolio page of her.

Manning appears to be getting the best deal, at least so far. The physical and mental abuse she underwent was not dissimilar to that of the hapless Abu Ghraib, Iraq, inmates in 2003. At the moment, Assange and Snowden have been spared the atrocities that Manning endured.

Snowden: The damned

Snowden lives in Russia, thanks to the kindness of the government there. Or should we should say he serves at the pleasure of President Putin. It's not hard to envision a deal between the Trump administration and Putin in which Snowden is sent back to the USA for some concessions to Russia. Maybe a few of the most pernicious sanctions lifted? Who knows?

John Young of Cryptome has found the slow pace of Snowden documents released thus far rediculous. He is right. Indeed, the overlords of the Snowden information have made sure that the drip, drip, drip of National Security Agency material have ensured the snail's pace for obvious reasons: Maintain MSM interest in Snowden; keep Snowden useful to Russian interests; and in appropriately mercenary fashion, keep readers interested in the journalists and publications that made their fame and fortune off of Snowden.

Snowden is "free" in a sense. But he is not "at home" and that obviously hurts him. If he leaves Russia he will be captured and returned to the USA to face prosecution. Like Assange, he has educated much of the public to the operations of the NSA and its counterparts. But how surprising were they, really? Intelligence and information are just two of the eight US instruments of national power.

There remains a cloud of suspicion over Snowden's motives, particularly since the Russians were not likely to take the heat for storing Snowden in their country without some notable return on the investment in him. That's just good business. But now the public relations gift of Snowden has started to slip dramatically for the Russians and they know it.

Manning and Snowden signed agreements with the US government to not reveal classified information. A price must be paid. And Assange knew he would piss off the US military, intelligence and diplomatic communities by posting sensitive information. The US will find, fix, track, target and capture Snowden and Assange as soon as an opportunity arises. Trade deals have been and are likely being discussed with Ecuador and Russia.

Meanwhile in the USA, Trump's press statements and his notorious Twitter messages are clearly damaging US government's institutions and agencies. The FBI, the Environmental Protection Agency, health care systems, the Justice Department, the Departments of Education and State are just some that have been the target of Trump's frothing at the mouth. His administration is understaffed and ill-tempered. callous even.

Snowden, Assange, Manning and Trump: When judgment day comes, and it will, who will have done the most damage to the United States of America?

WAR WITH NORTH KOREA: NO JOKE

April 28, 2017

The 20th century Korean War, from 1950–1953, pitting US-led United Nations coalition forces against the North Korean and Chinese militaries has been in pause mode for 64 years. The Korean Armistice was signed on July 27, 1953, by the United States, China and North Korea. It called for a cessation of hostilities until a lasting peace agreement between the warring parties could be negotiated and signed.

That, of course, has not happened due as much to North Korea's rationally maniacal behavior and ruthless treatment of its citizens, as to its role as a useful pawn of the Chinese, Russian and American governments. The Chinese feel compelled to let the incendiary North Korean government in Pyongyang irritate and provoke the United States and much of the world community, and the Americans don't mind having a large military presence to deter North Korea but also to keep an eye on the China and the Southeast Asian region.

China has apparently reinforced its military forces on its border with North Korea according to media reports.

Russia has a short land and maritime border with North Korea. In 2015, officials from the two countries signed an agreement to construct a road connection between the two neighbors during their "Year of Friendship." According to NK.News.org, North Korea and Russia envisioned "closer collaboration between the two states in political, economic and humanitarian spheres." As tensions ratchet up in the wake of North Korea's nuclear weapons and ballistic missile tests, Russia has apparently shored up its military forces near the bustling Russian port city of Vladivostok, home to Russia's Pacific Fleet and within range of North Korean missiles.

US-led coalition

These military moves by China and Russia make sense if war breaks out between a US-led coalition--that would likely include South Korea, Japan, Canada, and Australia (for starters), and North Korean forces. The extra forces would likely be used to stanch the tide of North Koreans expected to stream out of North Korea. In the unfortunate circumstance that sees North Korea's first use of a nuclear weapon, a US retaliatory strike would ensure that the radiologically damaged would seek care in China and Russia, care that China and Russia can ill-afford to provide on a large scale.

During a protracted conventional conflict, it seems likely that enterprising organizations in China and Russia would attempt to funnel weapons and aid to the North Koreans to keep the US-led coalition occupied while they ponder their strategic and tactical options. With the US bogged down in Iraq, Syria and Afghanistan, there are many moves that the Chinese and Russians could make contrary to US interests.

The political and pundit classes in New York City and Washington, DC, believe that the Trump administration will just kick the Kim Jong-Un tin can down the road for another US president. The same elites told us all that Hillary Clinton would, with great certainty, win the 2016 presidential election. After 100 days of the Trump presidency, they still shake their heads in disbelief. Yet, they seemed to believe fully in President Trump's punitive April cruise missile strikes in Syria undertaken after Bashar Al Assad's alleged use of a nerve agent on his own citizens. Americans live to fight, of course.

But Trump's people say that the time for "strategic patience" with North Korea is over. Secretary of State Rex Tillerson, the Perry Como of the US State Department, declared as much during a recent visit to South Korea. Has America's new Ken and Barbie, Jared Kushner and Ivanka Trump, been advising President Trump on the matter?

As for China's influence, it has warned North Korea not to test Trump even as it recently resumed flights to North Korea from Beijing. Time will tell if China is serious in assisting the US or not.

Intellectuals?

Beyond the political and pundit classes, who grace the world with their intellectual acumen, are those across the spectrum who think that North Korea is the way it is because of the policies and practices of the US government. Those outlandish claims should not be seriously entertained. Kim Jong-Un can be seen in a YouTube video smoking a cigarette, standing in the snow and watching his decrepit air force do fly bys. IN another he, sits at a desk, with an ashtray, watching his air force and army in action. It looks a lot like a Monty Python skit until you realize that the North Koreans really believe they are a competent military power. And then there is the North Korean Army's recent live fire exercises during which artillery pieces are tightly packed on a beach. What kind of commanders and political leaders think that the alignment of this artillery on a beach is a smart tactic? The commanders are essentially giving their troops a death sentence as US standoff weapons systems would mostly obliterate such massed artillery. North Korean military doctrine is as obsolete as much of its weaponry is.

Still, war is horrible and North Korea would, initially, likely cause a lot of pain to the northern portions of Seoul, South Korea. US, South and North Korean civilian casualties would certainly follow. Pain reduction, not elimination, depends on the lethality of US preemptive missile, bomber and cyber-attacks designed to neutralize what the US-led coalition's intelligence believes to be the targets most important to hit first. Most likely, both North Korean nuclear weapons testing and medium-long range missile sites would be targeted, simultaneously with other North Korean conventional military assets.

Before such a conflict, de-confliction lines with China and Russia would have to be opened.

The fight

North Korea has to know that if it moves any weapons systems into the open, the heat or electronic emissions will get them killed. US intelligence services have tried hard to anticipate how quickly the North Koreans can load and reload artillery and the extent of their ammunition supplies. Then there are the diesel submarines North Korea has in operation. US military anti-submarine warfare aircraft and detection is the best in the world and the Navy would be quick to begin the search for North Korean submarines. US attack class submarines would have to eliminate the DPRK's undersea threat very quickly, just as US air forces would be called upon to clear the airspace above North Korea as rapidly as possible. North Korean surface vessels would not do well against US anti-ship weaponry with its advanced guidance systems.

On the ground and from the sea, the situation is less clear. North Korea is vulnerable to amphibious landings on both its coastlines on the Yellow Sea and the Sea of Japan. The US Navy and Marine Corps would not attempt such landings until many days into a conflict though. North Korea is said to have sleeper cells in South Korea that would be activated to destroy key communications nodes and other critical infrastructure. North Korean Special Forces are said to be a dangerous threat as in any conflict they would be tasked with infiltrating South Korea to engage in sabotage.

It is not known how the North Korean civilian population would respond to an attack. The nation is home to 25 million people who have mostly known nothing but privation and austerity. Of course, that's the view from the outside. There are tantalizing hints that the civilians there might stay away from the fighting to a limited degree. Books smuggled out of North Korea like *The Accusation* give a hint of some of the thinking of the well-educated and economically better positioned denizens. But the US experience with insurgencies from Vietnam until the present have not been pleasant, successful affairs. At any rate, the "will" of the North Korean population would play a significant role in a protracted conflict.

Some argue that the US should learn from its 20th century Korean War experience. But comparisons are invalid. The conflict took place as the US was drawing down from World War II and cold political winds were blowing. Since that time, the North Koreans have spent a lot of time training to fight but have not been engaged in protracted conflicts for the last two decades as the US has been in Iraq and Afghanistan. There is no substitute for training but when military forces have experience in combat operations and also maintain a training regime, there is going to be an experience mismatch at some point favoring the US.

Yet another consideration is the Joint Force capabilities of the North Korean military versus the US coalition's interoperability and joint force training. There is no evidence to suggest that North Korea has "networked" its fighting forces to wage war in the cross domains of sea, undersea, land, air, space and cyber. Nor has North Korea conducted extensive training exercises with partner or allies equivalent to Canada, Australia, Japan and South Korea.

A long term conflict in which the US-led coalition fails to bring North Korea to its knees would allow other nations to make risky moves. Would Russia invade Eastern Ukraine and move up to the Dnieper River? Would China move on Taiwan? Would Turkey move further into Syria? Would Iran move further into Syria and Iraq? Would Russia get more aggressive in Libya?

Would Europe further splinter as some members of the European Union back the US while others do not (the UK would certainly fight with the US)?

Would the American public support a longer term war effort?

Unfortunately, the US, North and South Korea issue is unfinished business. Not too many people on the planet want to see a video of the Kim Jong-Un of the future sitting at his portable desk smoking a cigarette while watching the North Korean "Death to America" ICBM successfully launched and carrying a nuke toward the United States.

If that ICBM made in through US missile defenses, the United States nuclear retaliatory response would turn North Korea into a radiological waste-land for decades. No one in the world wants to see that happen either.

TRUMP UNLEASHES AMERICAN VERMIN, WAR DECLARED ON US SOCIETY

March 27, 2017

"I feel much alarmed at the prospect of seeing General Jackson President. He is one of the most unfit men I know of for such a place. He has had very little respect for laws and constitutions . . . His passions are terrible. When I was President of the Senate, he was Senator; and he could never speak on account of the rashness of his feelings. I have seen him attempt it repeatedly, and as often choke with rage. His passions are, no doubt, cooler now; he has been much tried since I knew him, but he is a dangerous man."—Thomas Jefferson

Jefferson held that a little revolution now and then in a democratic republic was a necessary evil, not unlike severe seasonal storms that come each year. Those storms can cause extensive damage to life and property but communities rally and rebuild. Often they develop improved protocols to deal with storms ranging from disaster response to revised building codes that might withstand the next big storm.

And yeah, Jefferson had black slaves like Jackson but, I mean, does that cancel out Jackson's madness and Jefferson's knowledge that the practice would destroy the United States? Who wants to relitigate those issues?

That said, Trump is the revolution that Jefferson predicted. And, like Jackson, Trump is a dangerous, non-calibrated human being. With the exception of Secretary of Defense Jim Mattis, Trump has loosed the bottom-feeders of America onto the American political scene. He has appointed extraordinarily wealthy individuals to cabinet positions with clear conflicts of interest who seek nothing less than the evisceration of the federal government's support for social welfare, culture, education and child care, plus the civilian federal workforce.

Kill every social program to tune of Climb Every Mountain

His destruction of the federal government is the long-standing goal of

America's most strident conservatives who want to see the role of the federal government limited to national security and law enforcement. It's part and parcel of the effort to destroy legacy programs established by Franklin D. Roosevelt such as Social Security.

Trump and his fellow vermin are undertaking these tasks with a gleeful vengeance normally reserved for autocratic governments. They are obscurantists and adhere to the script of Reich Minister of Propaganda Joseph Goebbels. ""It would not be impossible to prove with sufficient repetition and a psychological understanding of the people concerned that a square is in fact a circle. They are mere words, and words can be molded until they clothe ideas and disguise."

That could just as well have come out of former US Navy surface warfare officer and incendiary Steve Bannon.

The Trump folks proclaimed their support for state's rights during the 2016 campaign. They also claim that the federal government should not be meddling in citizen's freedom of choice. But their 2017 budget proposals and the health care plan would dump costs, responsibilities and choice issues onto state and local governments. Moreover, many states; for example, some energy dependent ones, do not have the funds to bolster either infrastructure repair or health care. In fact, many states are struggling to fully fund education programs.

Earlier in March, the Congressional Budget Office noted that millions of Americans would be left off the health insurance rolls under the Paul Ryan signature health care act. Remarkably, the conservative Freedom Caucus in the US House of Representatives believes Ryan's pogrom does not go far enough. They sought nothing less than clearing the way for the pillaging of the health care, education and Social Security programs.

And then there is Attorney General Jeff Sessions who wants to re-declare the drug war. This Republican believes state's rights do not matter as he claims he is going to crack down on marijuana usage.

Welcome to the French palace

Opioid addicts, coal miners, industrial workers, part-time workers, old and young are going to suffer mightily in the coming years. Trump's claims of making America Great Again ring hollow. Just glance at the resumes of the bulk of his Wall Street, politically connected cabinet. Has anyone of them spent time walking the streets of the rotting communities in West Virginia without a script and security detail.

Looking at President Trump and his court one can't help but think of the Frenchmen and women who marveled at the self-serving court of Louis the 16th and his wife Marie Antoinette.

I have written some vicious polemics over the years focusing on the Clintons, George W. Bush and Barack Obama. But Trump has gone far beyond his predecessors in his display of callousness, arrogance and rage aimed at over 55 percent of the American public. His distortion of facts, false promises and disparagement of allies, partners, congressional opposition, media, American citizens and, yes, corporations reeks of someone with vendetta against all those who mocked his political ambitions many years ago.

And the veiled racism in the repetitive attacks on Obama and Obamacare have become revolting. Trump and his cronies make sure to use the words failure and disaster at every turn as if on the 2016 campaign trail.

Steve Bannon has declared war on the press that is not on the right side of Trump, the New York Post reported. "It's not going to get better, it's going to get worse. They are adamantly opposed. Adamantly opposed to [the] economic nationalist agenda like Donald Trump has," said Bannon, who last month told the media to "keep its mouth shut." Nationalist economic program? What's next, Nationalist Socialism?

US storm troopers

Yes, Trump's stormtroopers have their day and are in charge. The Democrats, if they are to remain a viable long term party, must wage political war with their opponents. Playing nice will not work with Trump or the vermin he has released on the body politic. Americans opposed to Trump have to get off their butts and form a political party that can win major national offices and force the two parties to have to dilute the worst of their political platforms and people. Why not a party with the vigor of the US House Freedom Caucus? Where is the alt-Freedom Caucus in the House?

The seriousness of Trump's war on America is notable by its attack on the US intelligence machinery. Say what you will about the CIA, NSA, DIA, FBI NSA but the fact is they are needed to inhibit or prevent China, Russia and ISIS from creating havoc. Maybe some of their actions are unsavory but in a distasteful world, their services are necessary.

Trump and his campaign advisor and chair of the US House Intelligence Committee, David Nunes, has continued Trump's attack on the US intelligence community. On March 22, citing only sources, he announced that he had seen a transcript in which names were masked that indicated the NSA, under a court approved order, may have collected intelligence on Trump campaign people who were mentioned in conversations involving a foreign power (Update: Nunes charges were found to be baseless.)

Nunes is a Republican party stooge. He is young and seeks longevity in Congress and is betting on Ryan and Trump to increase his influence within the Republican party. Who leaked the classified information to him?

These Trump people are after us all. Quit pissing and moaning and do something.

THE DIGITAL STORM: BLOWING AWAY THE HUMAN MIND

March 1, 2017

"Temporal compression, as it is technically called, is an event that concretely modifies everyone's daily life at the same time. In the face of this acceleration of daily life, fear has become an environment even in a time of peace. We are living in the accident of the globe, the accident of instantaneous simultaneity and interactivity that have now gained the upper hand over ordinary activities . . . With the phenomena of instantaneous interaction that are now our lot, there has been a veritable reversal, destabilizing the relationship of human interactions and the time reserved for reflection in favor of the conditioned responses produced by emotion . . . Promoting progress means that we are always behind: on the high-speed Internet, on our Facebook profile, on our email inbox. There are always updates to be made: we are the objects of daily masochism and under constant tension."—The Administration of Fear, Paul Virillio

The electromagnetic/digital storm emanating from television, computer and cell phone screens flood the neural pathways of the brain drowning synapses. The ferocious digital winds from the storm twist and rattle axons, neurons and dendrites like the winds from a powerful thunderstorm that shears leaves off of trees and bends branches to and fro. The lightning strikes from this digital storm randomly sever connections in the cerebral cortex, just as a lightning strike violently amputates the limbs from a tree. And, at times, the electromagnetic field and its constituents, now having translated itself into images, sounds and text, crash into the cerebral cortex send shock waves through the entire structure of the brain down to the base of the spinal cord. The cerebral cortex has been trashed.

The new cocaine?

The digital storm, though ultimately damaging, is stimulating. It rushes to find the nucleus accumbens and floods it with dopamine which the hippocampus, in turn, 'memorizes' as rapid stimulus for satisfaction or pleasure. The amygdala then 'records' the event making sure that the human response is 'conditioned' to find pleasure and, indeed, seek it out desperately. The brain reboots itself and in so doing its human face. Addiction ensues and brains/humans change.

The digital storm forms a 'new brain' and, hence, human character. Transmogrification becomes complete. Perhaps it's all evolution's plan. But interesting symptoms appear indicating this could be devolution.

The addiction to the digital storm is so overwhelming that the brain creates a punishing craving mechanism: connection insecurity. Its emotion is fear, the fear of not being connected, or being seen, or taking part in the social scene. It's the fear of missing out on the daily online world and being MIA to comment on the latest incidental text, image or sound. To eliminate connection insecurity the brain creates an addiction that resembles the cocaine addict's frenzied search for more, having snorted up the buy and the stash.

Don't see me, touch me, read me

You can see it in the mothers and fathers that push their infant children down the sidewalk talking into the cell-phone rather than talking to the child. What does that child store in the brain? Gossip? Recipes? Sports trivia?

Or at the family dinner table where adults and children feel compelled to check email or take calls not wishing to be offline for 60 minutes at Sunday dinner. Worse still, the dinner hosts have to remind the cell-phone users to 'please silence your cell-phones' as if in the movie theater.

And walking down the street, the ability to say 'good morning or good evening' has been eroded as everyone seems to be working a conversation via the cell-phone or looking down at email. It's a world of people walking with their heads down on the street. It's heads down in elevators, offices and even in church pews on Sunday.

The brain's pause and contemplative thought functions have been degraded and exist like abandoned and rusty railroad tracks. The brain has replaced these two elements with a reflexive response mechanism from the unconscious and unfiltered mind.

Such is the mind of the president of the United States, Donald Trump and his penchant for Twitter, television and newspapers. His thinking, like the bulk of the American citizenry, is limited to 140 characters a thought. Producing 140 characters is an exhaustive effort for most these days. No doubt, a student has been assigned to describe the novel War and Peace in 140 characters. Tell us what is unique about your life in 140 characters, they'll ask.

And don't dare write an article of more than 500–750 words on a subject, because 'readers' will not stick with it, they say. 'Give me all bullet points,' our president says.

When falling asleep, or in your dreams, you 'see' text scrolling vertically/horizontally and you can actually read some of it. You can observe images of computer screens with data displayed, which you can interpret. Your brain and you are turning into a computer. And when you notice that these images start to appear in your recurring dreams and it seems to be altering your deepest consciousness, it's probably time to seek shelter from the digital storm. Think about it, if you can.

"'She watches with the raptor's eye, trained on distance as she is, and dark—so when she turns to what is close, so intimate and huge, she keeps the gift of sight beyond herself, neither sentimental or detached. . . . 'Who, indeed, watches the passing show with the raptor's eye? Couple the quick tweet and modalities of social networking with the videoing and blogging obsession, immersion in video games, overtime on the Internet and the constant interruption of face to face interaction by the cell phone, and you have a recipe for attention deficit in the life world. What are educational institutions to do in the culture of online engrossment and the fast electronic update? The humanities might rearticulate its worth in a climate of unexamined absorption."—A Field Guide to a New Meta-Field, Barbara Stafford

THE TRUMP CONUNDRUM

January 27, 2017

"We are free to believe that this is the century of authority, a century tending to the 'right,' a Fascist century. Now liberalism is preparing to close the doors of its temples, deserted by the peoples who feel that the agnosticism it professed in the sphere of economics and the indifferentism of which it has given proof in the sphere of politics and morals, would lead the world to ruin in the future as they have done in the past. This explains why all the political experiments of our day are anti-liberal, and it is supremely ridiculous to endeavor on this account to put them outside the pale of history, as though history were a preserve set aside for liberalism and its adepts; as though liberalism were the last word in civilization beyond which no one can go. Never before have the people thirsted for authority, direction, order, as they do now. If each age has its doctrine, then innumerable symptoms indicate that the doctrine of our age is the Fascist. Fascism respects the God of ascetics, saints, and heroes, and it also respects God as conceived by the ingenuous and primitive heart of the people, the God to whom their prayers are raised"—Benito Mussolini (1932)

OK, let's not be too hasty in comparing President Donald J. Trump to Mussolini. It is too soon for that as Pope Francis said recently.

But let us look very closely at what Trump's philosophy is while keeping an eye on Mussolini's musings in the snippet quoted above and in the president's diktats via Twitter. And let us pay attention to the political and economic landscape and the disaffection with neo-liberalism that is sweeping the Western World, and that appears to have ushered in an era belonging to the 'Alt-Right.'

Trump demands, not invites, corporations, unions—and both his supporters and critics—to begin the reindustrialization of America and a revitalization of the American 'spirit' and, as such, he appears to be closing the 'temple doors of liberalism.' He cited 'Almighty God' in his inaugural speech as a true friend of the United States and overlord of all that exists. Who knew?

President Trump's words and actions, thus far, point to a movement of the zealous religious-patriotic type that, if it is to succeed, must start with instilling a frenzied populist nationalism in the consciousness of most of America. Trump and staff members like Kellyanne Conway, Sarah Sanders and Sean Spicer (Update: fired by Trump) exhibit the zealotry of a once persecuted ideology and movement that now finds itself legitimized and holding the reins of power. Like Trump, the butt of criticism and satire for so long, they are overly defensive and create 'facts' that square with their vision and not necessarily reality.

The non-believers will pay

In Trump's America, enemies and blasphemers are the Republican and Democratic elites responsible for, or complicit in, replacing American labor with underpaid workers based in China, Mexico, India and the Philippines who have heretofore manufactured automobiles, cell phones and clothing. And the bad guys are those companies who have turned raw materials into airframes, computers and fiber optic cable abroad and then shipped them back to the US homeland free from import tariffs. It is federal, state and local governments who have allowed the American infrastructure—roads, bridges, rail, public education—to rot away. Those same governing levels sat idly by as the murder of civilians and law enforcement personnel took place.

Indeed, enemies may come to include those who choose not to follow the leader and dissent openly. Trump has said repeatedly that he will punish US corporations who manufacture overseas and then export finished goods to the USA by tax or tariff. What will be the penalty for those who challenge or question President Trump like CNN news? Pilloried, perhaps?

"Congratulations to @FoxNews for being number one in inauguration ratings. They were many times higher than FAKE NEWS @CNN—public is smart!, Trump opined in a Tweet on Jan. 24.

Will another House Committee on Un-American Activities subtly reemerge?

"I will be asking for a major investigation into VOTER FRAUD, including those registered to vote in two states, those who are illegal and even, those registered to vote who are dead (and many for a long time). Depending on results, we will strengthen up voting procedures!," Trump said in a Tweet on Jan. 25.

Trump has even blasted sacrosanct American aerospace and defense giants like Boeing and Lockheed for cost overruns on key aviation programs. Would Trump take it a notch higher if he knew that Boeing helps fund STEM education for Chinese students in China. Why not bring that money to the USA?

Now what? Diktat by Twitter

For years, critics of neo-liberalism (me too) have made the argument that the corporations that own the Republican and Democratic political parties were gutting the US Constitution, Bill of Rights and ideals contained in the Declaration of Independence. The 30 percent that own most of the wealth in America were enriching themselves at the expense of the remaining 70 percent, many who are only a few paydays from bankruptcy.

"The establishment protected itself, but not the citizens of our country. Their victories have not been your victories. Their triumphs have not been your triumphs. And while they celebrated in our nation's capital, there was little to celebrate for struggling families all across our land. That all changes starting right here and right now because this moment is your moment, it belongs to you," President Trump said during his inaugural speech on Jan. 20.

"Never before have the people thirsted for authority, direction, order, as they do now," said Mussolini.

Is President Donald Trump the Elmer Gantry of the Oval Office? Is he the Donald Trump fighting Don King in Celebrity Death Match on MTV? Is he a hypocrite that demeans the US federal government even as his Washington, DC, hotel is on a site that he leases from the US General Services Administration?

Or is he an American who seeks a better future for his grandchildren and all young Americans? It feels like the 1980s Ronald Reagan 'Morning in America' vibe in Washington, DC. But 2017 is radical, an acceleration of the cult of personality, conservatism and evangelical religion.

EMPEROR TWITTERITUS TRUMPARONIOUS: BIRTH ON TOTAL LUNAR ECLIPSE, 666 SIGNS

January 5, 2017

And so it came to pass that on the 1st month of the 20th day in the year of our Lord 2017, Emperor Twitteritus Trumparonious, born in the 6th month of the year of our Lord 1946, improbably snatched the reins of the glorious American Empire from Queen Hilliarious Clintoniosis whom the empire's military commanders, media propagandists, and many citizens hoped would rule over them. Queen Clintoniosis was guaranteed victory by all the most powerful soothsayers of the land and the court jesters of the day variously known as 'comedians and journalists'.

So it is recorded.

The political philistines labeled Trumparonious a buffoon, sorely lacking the appropriate temperament and manners to govern the most powerful Empire the Solar System has ever seen. Trumparonious had emerged from the dingy swamps of New York City's real estate underworld, conniving his way to fame and fortune. The Emperor fell hard too. His fame and fortune crumbled under him and he loathed having to meekly appeal, through his legal counselors, to the powerful money changers for credit.

But alas! The Emperor arose from the ashes, denounced his naysayers and joyfully entertained the Empire's citizens through television shows making many millions aware of the Trumparonious brand prior to his divine run for the seat of the American Empire.

Master

Little known to Queen Clintoniosis was that the Emperor was a master of the communications medium in all its forms and had many millions of followers who eagerly flocked to him. 'Experts' in the seats of power in Washington, DC, and New York City would come to decry these citizens as uncivilized and racist troglodytes who were best left to rot in West Virginia; Detroit and Flint, Michigan; and the baleful hinterlands of the Empire.

But, oh! Emperor Trumparonious came to the suffering in their hour of need and promised them rebirth and rejoicing if they would place their souls in his hands and elevate him to the throne. Those same souls had previously given themselves over to the Obamites, Busholites and to the Queen's husband, Emperor Billious.

And look! How Queen Clintoniosis, proconsuls, the rich and legions of the Empire did underestimate the Emperor Trumparonious. He now rules the land and the world!

And it came to pass that once on the throne, all of the Emperor's scurrilous enemies and vengeful 'experts' came to kiss his feet and ring at his tower kingdom in New York City. See how they endear themselves to him now, to serve the one they mocked as a fool. Who, now, has the last word?

Look at his disciples! How pure they are! Disciples worth billions and millions and some of the finest former military commanders from the Empire's legions now follow, work for him. Nay, the wealthiest should govern, should they not? Is this now not the world of Plato on whom the Emperor is the expert? And see how the Emperor is troubled by Plato's 5 regimes. He seeks Oligarchy but knows that the benefits of Tyranny are many, particularly law and order.

Would not Crassus of Rome rise from his grave if he could and praise the Emperor? Would not Crassus tell Emperor Trumapronious to turn on the disillusioned precariat of the land and crush them as he did to Spartacus and his minions?

Beast 666

The facts are these: The Emperor was born in the 6th month of the year in the 6th year of the 1940s. When in oration he moves his forefinger to the thumb making a circle with the other three digits in a vertical position revealing the 3rd six completing the beastly number 666. Further the Emperor was born on the 14th day of the 6th month of 1946, a day marked by a total lunar eclipse.

No one in the Empire dared utter the words, "The Emperor is the anti-Christ and his disciples the anti-Disciples." The foolhardy journalists who have questioned the Emperor's beliefs and judgement have come to a bitter end or have vanished.

And woe unto those who say that Putinious of Russia contributed to the Emperor's ascendancy! Look how the political philistines in the US Senate and House play their treacherous anti-Putinious game. A pox on their houses!

The Emperor is wise, indeed. Hundreds of gold plated statues of the Roman God Jupiter now dot city parks and community centers around the land. In 2017, Trumparonious decreed that Jupiter should be the state religion as it was through much of the Roman Empire. So it was written and so it was done.

But there were troubles and whispers of plots and conspiracies during the Emperor's rule. Perpetual wars and class, economic, and cultural fragmentation weighed on the minds of the citizens. But know this! The Emperor Trumparonious is studious and knows well of Caesar's end.

And it is said that someone with indestructible words caused the Emperor and his disciples to tremble in fear.

The one who said centuries ago, "Again I tell you, it is easier for a camel to go through the eye of a needle than for a rich person to enter the kingdom of God," returned.

It is not known how the Emperor fared and the direction history went.

GENERAL MARK MILLEY, CHIEF OF STAFF, US ARMY: THE IDEA OF AMERICA & WHY WE FIGHT

October 10, 2017, Courtesy Association of the US Army

Army Chief of Staff Gen. Mark A. Milley concluded a major speech at the association of the U.S. Army Annual Meeting and Exposition with what he called "a little commentary on why we fight."

Speaking at the Dwight David Eisenhower Luncheon where he and other chiefs have made major policy announcements about their visions for the Army's future, Milley said the U.S. was formed on a "very powerful idea … that here in America we will have a government of the people, by the people and for the people."

"It says that all of the people, regardless if you are male or female [are equal]," Milley said. "It doesn't matter if you are gay or straight or anything in between. It doesn't matter if you are black or white or Asian or Indian or any other ethnic group. It doesn't matter what the country of your origin is or the spelling of your last name. It does not matter if you are Catholic or Protestant, Muslim or Jew, and it doesn't matter if you believe at all."

"It does not matter if you are rich or poor, common or famous. In this country, in these United States, under these colors of red, white and blue, all Americans are created free and equal. We will rise or fall based on our merit, and we will be judged by the content of our character and not the color of our skin."

"That is the core organizing principle of the United States of America, and that is why we fight."